wok and stir fry

igloo

Published by Igloo Books Ltd
Cottage Farm
Sywell
NN6 0BJ
www.igloo-books.com

10 9 8 7 6 5 4 3 2 1

ISBN: 978 1 84817 631 7

Project Managed by R&R Publications Marketing Pty Ltd

Food Photography: R&R Photostudio (www.rrphotostudio.com.au)
Recipe Development: R&R Test Kitchen

Front cover photograph © Stockfood/Ian Garlick

Printed and manufactured in China

contents

introduction

The wok originated in China and is now the main cooking utensil in a number of Asian countries. It's also being used in many Western countries because of the unique way in which it cooks food.

In Indonesia, the wok is called a kuali or wajan. The Malay version is also a kuali, and in Vietnam it's called a chao. It's a cooking pan shaped like a large bowl with a rounded base to suit the large open fires originally used for cooking. Today there is a variety of woks available. There are flat based woks that are best suited to electric hotplates and electric woks that have a built in element. The general shape is the same in all woks, the wide open area being perfect for quick, even cooking of food.

The wok is one of the most versatile pieces of cooking equipment. It can be used for stir-frying, deep-frying, steaming, braising and boiling. For someone beginning to set up a kitchen, it's a great investment. The best woks are often inexpensive, and the more a wok is used, the better it is to cook in.

HOW TO STIR-FRY

Before you start stir-frying, you have to keep one thing in mind: speed is the most important element when stir-frying. Why? Because stir-frying is designed for quick cooking. This not only makes your food taste great it also preserves the colour and aroma of the ingredients. You always have to stir-fry on the highest heat possible – at the oil's smoking point to achieve the quickest stir-fry possible.

Follow these simple steps to the perfect stir-fry every time. 3–5 tablespoons of oil is recommended.

- Prepare your ingredients ahead of time. That includes washing and chopping them up.

- Add a good amount of oil into the wok; 3–5 tablespoons is recommended.

- Turn the heat on highest, and wait until the smoking point.

- Add any spices you have first, such as garlic, ginger, or chillies.

- Add your ingredients according to density. Always stir-fry meat first. If you plan to fry dense veggies such as broccoli or cauliflower, blanche or parboil them first.

- Add seasonings such as salt, sugar, hot sauce.

- Stir-fry to the point where the ingredients are just cooked, and no longer.

- Serve while hot. Follow these 8 simple stir-fry steps, and we guarantee you can stir-fry like a pro!

HOW TO CARE FOR YOUR WOK

Before using a new wok it's important to season it. First, wash it well with hot water and detergent to remove any coating. If the coating is a lacquer, fill the wok with cold water and 2 tablespoons of bicarbonate of soda and boil it for 15 minutes before removing the coating with a fine scourer.

The wok is then ready to be seasoned. To do this, place your wok over the heat, pour in 2 tablespoons of oil and add some chopped green onions and garlic cloves. Stir-fry these ingredients over a moderate heat for 2–3 minutes, covering the whole wok surface. Throw out the mixture and wash the wok in warm water. Wipe the wok out with paper towels and rub a fine film of oil over the inside. After seasoning a wok, never use anything abrasive to clean it. After every use, fill the wok with water, then wash it in soapy water. Always dry the wok well and wipe it out with a little oil before storing.

Cooking in a wok is good for quick family meals. It's also great for entertaining, because with stir-frying, most of the work is in the preparation and this can all be done in advance before the guests arrive.

This book will teach you the basic steps in preparing food that can be cooked in the wok. It will also help you with techniques you may not have tried before or are a little nervous about.

Asian cooking has been made popular by its delicious recipes and the quick and easy cooking method of stir-frying. Stir-frying lets you cook a variety of tasty recipes in minutes.

vegetable
stir-frys

Green Vegetable Stir-Fry with Sesame Seeds

(see photograph on page 8)

2 tablespoons sesame seeds

2 tablespoons peanut oil

1 clove garlic, roughly chopped

2½cm piece fresh ginger, finely chopped

150g broccoli, cut into very small florets

2 courgettes, halved lengthways and finely sliced

170g mange tout

1 tablespoon rice wine or medium-dry sherry

1 tablespoon dark soy sauce

1 tablespoon oyster sauce

1 Heat a wok. Add the sesame seeds and dry-fry for 2 minutes or until golden, shaking the pan frequently. Remove and set aside.

2 Add the oil to the wok, heat for 1 minute, then add the garlic and ginger and stir-fry over a medium heat for 1–2 minutes, until softened. Add the broccoli and stir-fry for a further 2–3 minutes.

3 Add the courgettes and mange tout and stir-fry for 3 minutes. Pour over the rice wine or sherry and sizzle for 1 minute. Add the soy and oyster sauces, mix well, then stir-fry for 2 minutes. Sprinkle over the fried sesame seeds just before serving.

Serves 4

Note: Dry-fry or toasted sesame seeds add a nutty taste to this quick and healthy Chinese dish. It's best to prepare all the vegetables before you start cooking.

Warm Spinach Salad with Walnuts

(see photograph opposite)

2 tablespoons walnut oil

5 sun-dried tomatoes in oil, drained and chopped

250g baby spinach

1 red onion, sliced into thin rings

2 tablespoons walnut pieces

salt

3 tablespoons chopped fresh coriander, to garnish

1 Heat the oil in a wok or large, heavy-based frying pan. Add the tomatoes, spinach, onion, walnut pieces and salt to taste. Cook for 1 minute or until the spinach begins to wilt, tossing to combine.

2 Transfer the vegetables to a large salad bowl and sprinkle with the coriander to garnish. Serve immediately.

Serves 4

Note: There's something seductive about warm salads – their flavours seem more intense. In this easy salad, walnuts, spinach and sun-dried tomatoes create a magical result.

Stir-Fry Bitter Melon

(see photograph opposite)

1 medium bitter melon (gourd), peeled, deseeded, cut into 1cm thick slices

2 tablespoons salt

1 teaspoon vegetable oil

3 tablespoons small dried prawns

6 shallots, sliced

2 cloves garlic, sliced

2 stalks fresh lemongrass, finely sliced, or 1 teaspoon finely grated lemon rind

3 fresh green chillies, finely sliced

1 small red papaya, cut into 3cm cubes

125g mange tout, halved

1 tablespoon tamarind concentrate

1 Rub each slice of bitter melon (gourd) with salt, place in a colander and set aside for 30 minutes. Rinse under cold water and drain thoroughly.

2 Heat the oil in a wok over a medium heat, add the dried prawns, French shallots, garlic and lemongrass or rind and stir-fry for 4 minutes or until the French shallots are golden.

3 Add the chillies and bitter melon (gourd) and stir-fry for 4 minutes or until the melon is tender. Add the pawpaw, snow peas and tamarind and stir-fry for 2 minutes or until the snow peas are tender.

Serves 4

Note: This dish is delicious served on a bed of cellophane noodles and topped with fried onions. Bitter melon (gourd) looks like a cucumber with a lumpy skin and, as the name suggests, has a bitter taste. It should always be degorged with salt before using.

Spinach with Sesame Seeds

700g fresh spinach, stalks removed

1 tablespoon peanut oil

1 teaspoon sesame oil

3 cloves garlic, chopped

2 tablespoons sesame seeds

juice of ½ lemon

¼ teaspoon finely grated lemon rind (optional)

salt and black pepper

1 Place the spinach in a large bowl, cover with boiling water, then leave for 2–3 minutes. Drain, then refresh under cold running water. Squeeze out any excess water, then coarsely chop.

2 Heat the peanut and sesame oils in a wok or large, heavy-based frying pan. Add the garlic and the sesame seeds and fry for 1–2 minutes, until the garlic begins to brown and the seeds start to pop.

3 Stir in the spinach and fry for 1–2 minutes, until heated through. Add the lemon juice and rind, if using, then season and mix well.

Serves 6

Note: Lemony spinach adds a refreshing tang to roast meat and fish dishes. It can also make a substantial snack with poached eggs and bread.

Wilted Rocket Cheese Salad

3 tablespoons olive oil

4 slices white bread, crusts removed and cut into cubes

3 spring onions, sliced diagonally

2 cloves garlic, crushed

2 courgettes, cut lengthwise into thin strips

1 red pepper, thinly sliced

½ cup raisins

250g rocket

125g blue cheese, crumbled

2 tablespoons balsamic vinegar

1 Heat 2 tablespoons of oil in a wok over a medium heat, add the bread and stir-fry for 3 minutes or until golden. Drain on absorbent paper.

2 Heat the remaining oil in the wok, add the spring onions and garlic and stir-fry for 2 minutes. Add the courgettes, peppers and raisins and stir-fry for 3 minutes or until the vegetables are just tender. Remove them from the wok and set aside.

3 Add the rocket to the wok and stir-fry for 2 minutes or until just wilts. Place the rocket on a serving platter or divide between individual bowls or plates, then top with the vegetable mixture and scatter with the croûtons and blue cheese. Drizzle with the balsamic vinegar and serve immediately.

Serves 4

Note: If rocket is unavailable this salad is also delicious made with English spinach or watercress.

Mange Tout and Mango Stir-Fry

300g mange tout, trimmed

1 onion, cut into rings

1 clove garlic, chopped

1 tablespoon peanut oil

2 tablespoons chopped fresh ginger

440g can mangoes in juice

¼ cup roasted peanuts, to garnish

1 Heat the oil in a wok or large frying pan. Stir-fry the onion, garlic and ginger until the onion is clear. Add the mange tout and stir for 2–3 minutes. Drain the mangoes, reserving ¼ cup of juice.

3 Cut the mangoes into slices. Add the reserved juice and mangoes to the wok. Cover and cook for 3–5 minutes or until the mange touts are just tender. Garnish with the peanuts.

Serves 4

Aubergine and Basil Stir-Fry

3 aubergines, halved lengthways and cut into 1cm thick slices

salt to taste

1 tablespoon vegetable oil

2 onions, cut into thin wedges, layers separated

3 fresh red chillies, chopped

2 cloves garlic, sliced

1 stalk fresh lemongrass, chopped, or ½ teaspoon dried lemongrass, soaked in hot water until soft

250g green beans, trimmed

1 cup coconut cream

45g basil leaves

1 Place the aubergines in a colander, sprinkle with salt and set aside for 20 minutes. Rinse under cold running water and pat dry on absorbent paper.

2 Heat the oil in a wok over a high heat, add the onions, chillies, garlic and lemongrass and stir-fry for 3 minutes. Add the aubergine, beans and coconut cream and stir-fry for 5 minutes or until the eggplant is tender. Stir in the basil just before serving.

Serves 6

Oriental Green Bean Stir-Fry

1 tablespoon sesame oil

500g baby green beans

2 teaspoons light soy sauce

2 teaspoons toasted sesame seeds

2 tablespoons toasted flaked almonds

1 spring onion, thinly sliced

1 Heat a wok and pour in the oil. Add the beans and stir-fry for 1–2 minutes. Add the soy sauce, sesame seeds, almonds and spring onion, and stir-fry for a further 1 minute. Serve immediately.

Serves 2–4

Note: Use whole baby green beans for this dish and serve it as an entrée or a vegetable accompaniment. A delicious variation is to use fresh young asparagus when it's in season, instead of the beans.

Pak Choi in Oyster Sauce

400g pak choi

3 tablespoons oyster sauce

1 tablespoon peanut oil

salt

1 Trim the ends of the pak choi stalks, then separate the leaves and rinse thoroughly. Mix together the oyster sauce and oil.

2 Put the pak choi into a wok of lightly salted boiling water and cook, uncovered, for 3 minutes or until tender. Drain thoroughly, return the pak choi to the wok, then add the oyster sauce and oil mixture and toss to coat evenly.

Serves 4

Tofu Stir-Fry

2 tablespoons peanut oil

1 clove garlic, finely chopped

1 teaspoon finely chopped ginger

1 red onion, sliced

125g thinly sliced celery

1 red peppr

1 carrot, cut into julienne strips

125g green beans, blanched

75g broccoli florets, blanched

2 tablespoons light soy sauce

3 tablespoons dry sherry

1 teaspoon caster sugar

125g mange tout

250g firm tofu, cubed

1   Heat the oil in a wok or large frying pan, add the garlic, ginger and onion and stir-fry over a high heat for 1 minute. Add the celery, capsicum, carrot, beans and broccoli and stir-fry for 3 minutes.

2   Mix the soy sauce, sherry and sugar together in a bowl and add to the vegetables along with the mange tout and tofu. Stir-fry for a further 2 minutes and serve immediately with steamed or boiled rice.

Serves 2

Green Vegetable Stir-Fry

1 tablespoon oil

1 onion, sliced

1 teaspoon grated ginger

1 teaspoon crushed garlic

2 teaspoons Thai green curry paste

500g assorted sliced green vegetables:
broccoli, mange tout, beans, spinach

2 teaspoons chopped coriander

1 tablespoon Thai fish sauce (nam pla)

2 tablespoons finely shredded kaffir
lime leaves (optional)

1 Heat the oil in a wok over a medium heat. Add the onion, ginger, garlic and curry paste and fry for 2–3 minutes.

2 Add the green vegetables and toss over the heat for 2–3 minutes, until bright green. Add the, coriander, fish sauce and lime leaves (if using), mix well and toss over the heat for 1–2 minutes. Serve with rice and stir-frys or with plain meat dishes.

Serves 4

Warm Vegetable Salad

(see photograph opposite)

1 tablespoon vegetable oil

125g blanched hazelnuts

2 onions, chopped

2 carrots, sliced

2 courgettes, chopped

145g mange tout

4 field mushrooms, sliced

1 green and red peper, sliced

6 spring onions, chopped

250g asparagus, halved

RED WINE AND THYME VINAIGRETTE

⅓ cup olive oil

¼ cup vinegar

1 tablespoon chopped fresh thyme

1 teaspoon sugar

freshly ground black pepper

1 To make the vinaigrette, place the olive oil, vinegar, thyme, sugar and black pepper to taste in a screwtop jar and shake well to combine. Set aside.

2 Heat ½ tablespoon vegetable oil in a wok over a high heat, add the hazelnuts and stir-fry for 3 minutes. Set aside. Heat the remaining oil in the wok, add the onions and stir-fry for 3 minutes or until golden.

3 Add the carrots, courgettes, mange tout, mushrooms, peppers, spring onions and asparagus and stir-fry for 5 minutes. Return the hazelnuts to the wok, add the vinaigrette and toss to combine.

Serves 4

Tofu with Peaches and Mange Tout

370g tofu

55g flour, seasoned

3 tablespoons oil

1 large onion, cut into rings

1cm piece fresh ginger root, peeled

1 clove garlic

300g mange tout, topped and tailed

⅓ cup dry white wine

200g packet dried peaches

3 teaspoons soy sauce

2 teaspoons sugar

1   Cut the tofu into 6 cubes and toss with the seasoned flour.

2   Heat the oil in a wok and fry the onion rings until golden. Remove.

3   Add the ginger and garlic, fry for 30 seconds to flavour the oil, then remove. Add the tofu cubes and fry, turning with tongs, until golden on all sides. Remove and drain on kitchen paper.

4   Fry the mange tout for about 1 minute or to desired crispness. Remove.

5   Pour the wine into the wok and add the peaches. Simmer for1 minute; turn the peaches. Add the soy sauce and sugar. Mix into wok. Pile the tofu, mange tout and peaches onto plates. Pour the sauce over and top with the onion rings

Serves 2–3

Tofu, Broccoli and Wilted Spinach Stir-Fry

1 head broccoli

250g tofu

2 cloves garlic

1 tablespoon grated root ginger

2 tablespoons sesame oil

1 teaspoon prepared minced chilli

1 tablespoon oil

about 12 spinach leaves

about 12 brown button mushrooms

2 tablespoons vegetarian stir-fry sauce

1 tablespoon soy sauce

2 teaspoons black sesame seeds

2 teaspoons sesame seeds

4 cups cooked rice

1 Wash broccoli and cut into florets. Microwave on high power for 1½ minutes or blanch in boiling water for 2 minutes. Drain and set aside.

2 Drain tofu and cut into 2cm pieces. Crush, peel and finely chop garlic. Mix garlic, ginger, sesame oil and minced chilli together in a medium-sized bowl. Add tofu and mix gently to coat the tofu. Leave to marinate for 30 minutes or, if time is short, cook straight away.

3 Heat oil in a wok or large frying pan. Add tofu and stir-fry for 4 minutes until browned on all sides, taking care not to break up the tofu.

4 Wash spinach and shake off excess water. Wipe mushrooms and cut in half. Add spinach, mushrooms and broccoli to wok for 2 minutes.

5 Mix stir-fry and soy sauces together. Add to wok and stir-fry to combine. Serve on a bed of rice, garnished with black and hulled sesame seeds.

Serves 4

chicken and poultry stir-frys

Ginger and Lemon Chicken Stir-Fry

(see photograph on page 26)

finely grated rind and juice of 1 lemon

2 cloves garlic, crushed

2 tablespoons chopped fresh coriander

black pepper

340g skinless boneless chicken breasts,
  cut into strips

2 tablespoon sesame seeds

1 tablespoon sesame oil

2½cm piece fresh ginger, finely
  chopped

2 carrots, cut into matchsticks

1 leek, thinly sliced

170g mange tout

125g bean sprouts

1 tablespoon dry sherry

1 tablespoon light soy sauce

1 In a non-metallic bowl, mix the lemon rind and juice, half the garlic, and the coriander. Season with black pepper and add the chicken. Stir to coat the chicken, then cover and refrigerate for 1 hour.

2 Heat a non-stick wok or large frying pan and dry-fry the sesame seeds for 30 seconds, stirring well. Remove and set aside. Add the oil to the wok or pan, heat, then stir-fry the ginger and remaining garlic for 30 seconds. Add the chicken and marinade and stir-fry for 4 minutes.

3 Add the carrots and leek and stir-fry for 1–2 minutes. Add the mange tout and bean sprouts and stir-fry for 2–3 minutes, until everything is tender. Pour in the sherry and soy sauce and sizzle for 1–2 minutes, then sprinkle over the sesame seeds.

Serves 4

Note: The aroma of ginger, coriander and soy sauce will whet the appetites of your family and friends. Make sure you don't overcook the vegetables – they should still be quite crunchy.

Sweet and Sour Chicken

(see photograph opposite)

400g can pineapple pieces

1 red pepper, deseeded

6 spring onions

2 teaspoons soy sauce

2 tablespoons malt vinegar

2 tablespoons brown sugar

1 tablespoon lemon juice

1 teaspoon finely grated fresh ginger

2 tablespoons tomato sauce

1 tablespoon cornflour

2 tablespoons water

500g chicken thigh fillets

3 tablespoons oil

1 Drain the pineapple pieces and reserve the juice. Cut the pepper into strips or squares. Cut the spring onions, including most of the green shoot, into 1cm diagonal pieces. Mix together the pineapple juice, soy sauce, vinegar, sugar, lemon juice, ginger and tomato sauce. Blend the water and cornflour and set aside. Cut each thigh fillet into 1cm wide strips.

2 Heat the wok, add 2 tablespoons of oil and, when hot, add a third of the chicken. Stir-fry over a high heat until cooked, about 1 minute. Remove and cook the remaining chicken in 2 batches, adding extra oil if needed. Drain the chicken well on absorbent paper. Drain all oil from the wok.

3 Pour the sauce mixture into the wok and add the blended cornflour. Cook, stirring, until the mixture boils and thickens. Stir in the pepper, spring onions and pineapple pieces and cook for 1 minute. Add the chicken and heat through. Serve immediately with boiled rice.

Serves 6

Chicken with Capsicums and Chilli Garlic Sauce

(see photograph opposite)

500g chicken breast

1 green pepper

1 red pepper

1 yellow pepper

3 spring onions

2 tablespoons sesame oil

¼ cup chilli garlic sauce

2 tablespoons water

4 cups cooked rice

1 Trim chicken pieces, removing any excess fat and cutting into even-sized pieces. Cut peppers in half, remove core and seeds and cut flesh into 1cm strips. Trim spring onions and cut into 2cm pieces on the diagonal.

2 Heat oil in a wok or large frying pan. Stir-fry peppers and spring onions for 2 minutes. Remove from wok and set aside.

3 Add chicken to wok and stir-fry for 3–4 minutes or until cooked. Mix chilli garlic sauce and water together. Return peppers and spring onions to wok and pour sauce mixture over. Serve with rice.

Serves 4

Note: Chilli sauce is a superb product to have in your pantry – it's versatile and packed with flavour.

Samosas

(see photograph opposite)

1 tablespoon vegetable oil

2 medium onions, finely chopped

1 clove garlic, crushed

2 teaspoons curry paste

½ teaspoon salt

1 tablespoon white vinegar

250g chicken mince

½ cup water

2 teaspoons sweet chilli sauce

2 tablespoons coriander, chopped

1 packet frozen spring roll wrappers

1½ cups vegetable oil

1   Heat the wok, add the oil and fry the onions and garlic until the onions are soft. Add the curry paste and salt and fry a little (about 30 seconds). Stir in the vinegar. Add the chicken mince and stir-fry on high until the chicken changes colour. Break up any lumps. Reduce heat, add the water, cover and cook until most of the water is absorbed (about 6 minutes). Uncover, and add the chilli sauce and coriander. Stir until the water has evaporated and the chicken is dry. Remove to a plate to cool. Rinse the wok.

2   Cut 10 spring roll wrappers into 3 even pieces 7½ x 20cm. Place a teaspoon of filling at bottom end and fold over the pastry diagonally, forming a triangle. Fold again on the straight. Continue to make 3 more folds in same way. Moisten the inside edge of the last fold with water and press gently to seal.

3   Heat the clean wok. Add about 5cm of oil. Heat the oil but take care not to overheat. Add 3–4 samosas and fry until golden. Remove with a slotted spoon to a tray lined with absorbent paper. Repeat with the remainder. If the samosas become dark in colour, immediately remove them from the heat to drop the oil temperature.

Makes 30–36

Chicken Rogan Josh

(see photograph opposite)

8 skinless boneless chicken thighs

1 tablespoon vegetable oil

1 small red and 1 small green pepper, deseeded and thinly sliced

1 onion, thinly sliced

5cm piece of fresh ginger, finely chopped

2 cloves garlic, crushed

2 tablespoons garam masala

1 teaspoon each paprika, turmeric and chilli powder

4 cardamom pods, crushed

salt

200g Greek yoghurt

400g can chopped tomatoes

fresh coriander, to garnish

1 Cut each thigh into 4 pieces. Heat the oil in a large heavy-based frying pan and add the peppers, onion, ginger, garlic, spices and a good pinch of salt. Fry over a low heat for 5 minutes or until the peppers and onion have softened.

2 Add the chicken to the pan, then add 2 tablespoons of the yoghurt. Increase the heat to medium and cook for 4 minutes or until the yoghurt is absorbed. Repeat the step above until all yoghurt is used.

3 Increase the heat to high, stir in the tomatoes and 200ml of water and bring to the boil. Reduce the heat, cover, and simmer for 30 minutes or until the chicken is tender, stirring occasionally and adding more water if the sauce becomes too dry.

4 Uncover the pan, increase the heat to high and cook, stirring constantly, for 5 minutes or until the sauce thickens. Garnish with coriander.

Serves 4

Fragrant Duck with Pineapple

(see photograph opposite)

2 boneless duck breasts, about 175g each, skinned and cut into strips

1 teaspoon five spice powder

2 tablespoons soy sauce

2 tablespoons rice wine or dry sherry

1 teaspoon sugar

1 tablespoon peanut oil

1 orange or red pepper, deseeded and cut into thin strips

5cm piece fresh ginger, cut into matchsticks

2 spring onions, white and green parts separated, thinly shredded

170g fresh pineapple, cut into bite-size pieces, plus juice

salt

1 Place the duck, five spice powder, soy sauce, rice wine or sherry and sugar in a shallow non-metallic bowl. Cover and marinate for 20 minutes.

2 Heat the oil in a wok. Remove the duck from the marinade and reserve. Stir-fry the duck over a high heat for 2 minutes. Add the pepper, ginger and the white spring onion parts and stir-fry for a further 3–4 minutes, until the capsicum starts to soften.

3 Add the pineapple and juice and the marinade. Stir-fry for 1–2 minutes. Season with salt if desired. Serve immediately, sprinkled with the green spring onion parts.

Serves 4

Note: Fresh pineapple cuts through the richness of tender duck breasts marinated in Chinese spices. Serve this dish with plain boiled noodles or some fragrant Thai rice.

Japanese Pan-Fry Glazed Chicken

1 tablespoon peanut oil

4 skinless boneless chicken breasts,
  sliced diagonally

spring onions, shredded, to garnish

GLAZE

⅓ cup Japanese or other dark soy sauce

⅓ cup rice wine or medium-dry sherry

3 tablespoons granulated sugar

1 Heat the oil in a large, heavy-based frying pan. Fry the chicken for
   3–5 minutes, until lightly coloured. Pour over the glaze.

2 Fry for 5 minutes or until the glaze has nearly evaporated and the chicken
   pieces are coated and cooked through, turning them occasionally. Serve
   garnished with spring onions.

GLAZE

1 Place the soy sauce, rice wine or sherry and the sugar into a small saucepan.
   Cook gently, stirring, for 3 minutes or until the sugar has dissolved.

Serves 4

*Note: In Japan, this sweet glazed dish is known as teriyaki. The recipe works
equally well with beef or pork and is traditionally served with rice.*

Braised Chicken Wings

1 kg chicken wings

2 tablespoons peanut oil

4 tablespoons soy sauce

2 tablespoons honey

grated zest of 1 lemon

2 tablespoons dry sherry

1 clove garlic, chopped

2½cm piece of fresh root ginger, grated

1   Using a sharp knife, remove the wing tips from the chicken wings and cut each wing in half at the joint.

2   Heat a wok and pour in the oil. When the oil is very hot, add the wings and stir-fry for 3–4 minutes. Stir in the soy sauce, honey, lemon rind, sherry and garlic. Keep stirring until the liquid comes to the boil.

3   Cover the wok with a tight-fitting lid and reduce the heat. Simmer the wings over a gentle heat for 30 minutes or until tender. Stir occasionally to stop the sauce from sticking, especially towards the end of the cooking time.

Serves 4

Thai-Spiced Chicken with Courgette

(see photograph opposite)

1 tablespoon olive oil

1 clove garlic, finely chopped

2½cm piece fresh ginger, finely chopped

1 small fresh red chilli, deseeded and finely chopped

350g skinless boneless chicken breasts, cut into strips

1 tablespoon Thai 7-spice seasoning

1 red and 1 yellow pepper, deseeded and sliced

2 courgette, thinly sliced

215g can bamboo shoots, drained

2 tablespoons dry sherry or apple juice

1 tablespoon light soy sauce

black pepper

2 tablespoons chopped fresh coriander, plus extra to garnish

1 Heat the oil in a non-stick wok or large frying pan. Add the garlic, ginger and chilli and stir-fry for 30 seconds to release the flavours.

2 Add the chicken and Thai seasoning and stir-fry for 4 minutes or until the chicken has coloured. Add the peppers and courgettes and stir-fry for 1–2 minutes, until slightly softened.

3 Stir in the bamboo shoots and stir-fry for another 2–3 minutes, until the chicken is cooked through and tender. Add the sherry or apple juice, soy sauce and black pepper and sizzle for 1–2 minutes. Remove from the heat and stir in the chopped coriander, then garnish with more coriander.

Serves 4

Note: This stir-fry is quick to make and tastes sensational. It helps if you prepare all the vegetables in advance and keep the wok really hot. Serve with rice or noodles.

Stir-Fry Duck with Greens

1 kg Chinese barbecued or roasted duck

2 teaspoons vegetable oil

1 tablespoon Thai red curry paste

1 teaspoon prawn paste

1 stalk fresh lemongrass, finely sliced, or ½ teaspoon dried lemongrass, soaked in hot water until soft

4 fresh red chillies

1 bunch Chinese broccoli or Swiss chard, chopped

1 tablespoon palm or brown sugar

2 tablespoons tamarind concentrate

1 tablespoon Thai fish sauce (nam pla)

1 Slice the meat from the duck, leaving the skin on, and cut it into bite-size pieces. Reserve as many of the cavity juices as possible.

2 Heat the oil in a wok over a medium heat, add the curry paste, prawn paste, lemongrass and chillies and stir-fry for 3 minutes or until fragrant.

3 Add the duck and the reserved juices and stir-fry for 2 minutes or until coated in the spice mixture and heated. Add the broccoli or chard, sugar, tamarind and fish sauce and stir-fry for 3–4 minutes or until the broccoli is wilted.

Serves 4

Note: Chinese broccoli is a popular Asian vegetable. It has dark green leaves on firm stalks, often with small white flowers. The leaves, stalks and flowers are all used in cooking, however the stalks are considered the choicest part of the plant. To prepare, remove the leaves from the stalks and peel, then chop both the leaves and the stalks.

Green Banana Chicken Curry

1 teaspoon salt

1 teaspoon ground turmeric

10 green bananas, peeled

2 tablespoons vegetable oil

3 spring onions, chopped

1 tablespoon finely grated fresh ginger

2 small fresh red chillies, deseeded
and chopped

1½ cups coconut milk

1 cinnamon stick

45g sultanas

30g roasted cashews

6 chicken breast fillets, cut into thin
strips

1 Combine the salt and turmeric and rub over the bananas.

2 Heat the oil in a wok over a medium heat, add the bananas and stir-fry for
5 minutes or until brown. Remove the bananas from the pan and drain on
absorbent paper.

3 Add the spring onions, ginger and chillies to the pan and stir-fry for 2 minutes
or until the mixture is soft. Stir in the coconut milk, cinnamon, sultanas,
cashews and chicken and bring to simmering. Simmer, stirring occasionally,
for 20 minutes.

4 Slice the bananas, return to the pan and simmer, stirring occasionally,
for 10 minutes or until the chicken is tender. Remove the cinnamon stick
before serving.

Serves 6

Chicken Stir-Fry with Lemon and Mango

(see photograph opposite)

1 ripe mango

2 tablespoons sunflower oil

2 garlic cloves, crushed

2½cm piece fresh ginger, finely chopped

4 chicken breast fillets, cut into strips

150g mange tout, halved lengthways

2 celery sticks, thinly sliced

1 yellow pepper, deseeded and cut into matchsticks

4 spring onions, thinly sliced

sea salt and freshly ground black pepper

juice of ½ lemon

2 tablespoons white wine or apple juice

1 tablespoon balsamic vinegar

1 tablespoon clear honey

2 tablespoons chopped fresh coriander

1 Slice the two fatter 'cheeks' of the mango from either side of the stone. Cut a criss-cross pattern across the flesh of each piece to separate it into small cubes, then push the skin upwards and slice off the cubes. Set aside.

2 Heat the oil in a wok or large frying pan until hot. Add the garlic, ginger and chicken and stir-fry for 3 minutes.

3 Add the mange tout, celery and pepper and stir-fry for 3–4 minutes. Add the spring onions, mango and seasoning, then stir-fry for a further 2 minutes.

4 Combine the lemon juice with the white wine or apple juice, balsamic vinegar and honey in a small bowl. Add to the wok and continue to cook for 2 minutes. Add the coriander and serve.

Serves 6

Creamy Chicken Korma

3 tablespoons vegetable oil

1 onion, chopped

2 cloves garlic, crushed

3 tablespoons plain flour

2 tablespoons mild korma curry powder

750g skinless boneless chicken breasts,
cut into 2½cm cubes

1½ cups chicken stock

30g raisins

1 tablespoon chopped fresh coriander

1 teaspoon garam masala

juice of ½ lemon

4 tablespoons sour cream

1   Heat the oil in a wok, add the onion and garlic and cook gently for
5 minutes or until softened.

2   Mix the flour and curry powder in a bowl. Toss the chicken in the seasoned
flour, coating well. Reserve the flour. Add the chicken to the onion and garlic,
then cook, stirring, for 3–4 minutes, until lightly browned. Stir in the seasoned
flour and cook for 1 minute.

3   Add the stock and raisins and bring to the boil, stirring. Cover and simmer for
15 minutes. Add the coriander and garam masala and cook for a further
5 minutes or until the flavours are released and the chicken is cooked
through. Remove the wok from the heat and stir in the lemon juice and
sour cream. Return to the heat and warm through, taking care not to let the
mixture boil.

Serves 4

Turkey and Mushroom Creole

1 tablespoon olive oil

1 onion, chopped

2 cloves garlic, chopped

1 red capsicumpepperped

2 sticks celery, chopped

400g can chopped tomatoes

1 teaspoon chilli powder

large pinch of cayenne pepper

1 teaspoon paprika

¼ teaspoon dried thyme

500g quick-cook turkey steaks, cut into strips

125g button mushrooms, sliced

1 Heat the oil in a wok, then add the onion, garlic, pepper and celery and cook gently for 10 minutes or until softened.

2 Stir in the tomatoes, chilli, cayenne, paprika and thyme and heat through for 1–2 minutes to release the flavours. Stir in the turkey and mushrooms, then cover the wok and cook gently for 30 minutes, stirring occasionally, until the turkey is cooked through and tender.

Serves 4

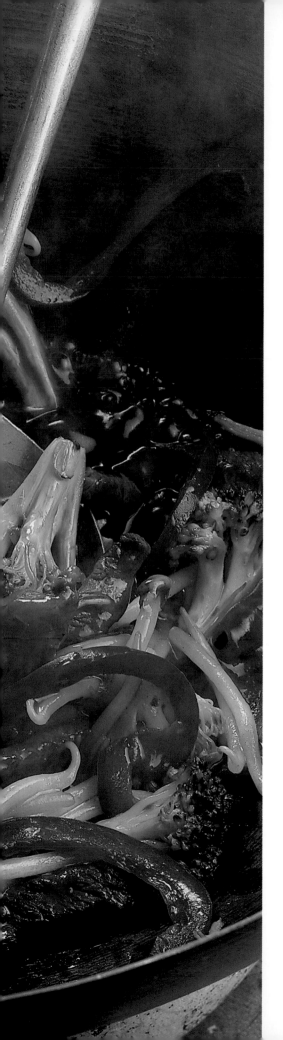

meat stir-frys

Sizzling Beef

(see photograph on page 48)

500g rump steak, trimmed of any
  excess fat and cut into thin strips

2 tablespoons soy sauce

2 tablespoons rice wine or sherry

1½ tablespoon cornflour

1 teaspoon sugar

3 tablespoons peanut oil

145g broccoli, cut into bite-size pieces

1 large red pepper, deseeded and cut
  into thin strips

2 cloves garlic, crushed

3 tablespoons oyster sauce

200g pack fresh bean sprouts

salt and black pepper

1 Put the steak, soy sauce, rice wine or sherry, cornflour and sugar into a non-metallic bowl and mix thoroughly.

2 Heat 1 tablespoon of the oil in a wok or large heavy-based frying pan, add a third of the beef mixture and stir-fry over a high heat for 2–3 minutes, until browned. Remove and cook the remaining beef in 2 more batches, adding a little more oil if necessary.

3 Heat the remaining oil in the wok, then add the broccoli and 6 tablespoons of water. Stir-fry for 5 minutes, then add the pepper and garlic and stir-fry for a further 2–3 minutes, until the broccoli is tender but still firm to the bite.

4 Stir in the oyster sauce, return the beef to the wok and add the bean sprouts. Toss over a high heat for 2 minutes or until the beef is piping hot and the bean sprouts have softened slightly, then season.

Serves 4

Note: Before you start cooking this colourful stir-fry, make sure all your ingredients are cut into pieces of roughly the same shape and size so they cook evenly.

Keema Curry

(see photograph opposite)

1 tablespoon vegetable oil

1 onion, finely chopped

2½cm piece fresh ginger, grated

2 cloves garlic, crushed

500g lean minced lamb

2 teaspoons ground turmeric

1 teaspoon chilli powder

1 tablespoon garam masala

3 tablespoons tomato purée

2 cups lamb stock

125g frozen peas

2 tablespoons chopped fresh coriander,
  plus extra leaves to garnish

salt and black pepper

1 Heat the oil in a large heavy-based frying pan. Add the onion and ginger and cook over a low heat for 5 minutes or until softened. Add the garlic and minced lamb, breaking the meat into little pieces by pressing it with the back of a wooden spoon. Cook for 10 minutes or until the lamb browns.

2 Pour off any excess fat from the pan. Add the turmeric, chilli, garam masala and tomato purée, then stir-fry for 1–2 minutes. Add the stock and bring to the boil, stirring, then reduce the heat and simmer, uncovered, for 10 minutes or until slightly reduced.

3 Add the peas, then simmer for 5–10 minutes longer. Remove from the heat, stir in the coriander and season. Garnish with the extra coriander.

Serves 4

Note: This is a really easy way to turn minced lamb into a delicious spicy curry. It's best served the traditional way – with basmati rice, cucumber raita and mango chutney.

Pork Chop Suey

500g diced pork

3 cups sliced mixed fresh vegetables

100g peeled green prawns

1 large onion, sliced

1cm fresh peeled ginger, finely chopped

3 tablespoons olive oil

4 teaspoons freshly crushed garlic

fresh sliced spring onions, to garnish

1 Bring water to a rapid boil in a frying pan.

2 Add the fresh vegetables and blanch, over a high heat, for 2 minutes. Drain, cool under cold water and drain again.

3 Heat the oil in a frying pan over a medium heat and cook the prawns until they just turn pink. Remove. Add the pork and sauté it with the onion, garlic and ginger until pork is cooked, about 5 minutes.

4 Add a little extra oil if necessary and toss through the blanched vegetables. Reduce the heat to low, add the combined sauce ingredients and stir until thickened.

5 Return the prawns to the frying pan and simmer for 1 minute. Garnish with spring onions and serve with hot steamed rice.

Serves 4

Mongolian Lamb

2 teaspoons vegetable oil

500g lamb fillet, cut into paper-thin slices

2 onions, cut into 8 wedges

4 spring onions, chopped

3 cloves garlic, crushed

2 small fresh red chillies, deseeded and chopped

1 tablespoon chopped fresh coriander

MONGOLIAN SAUCE

2½ teaspoons cornflour

1½ tablespoons light soy sauce

1 tablespoon oyster sauce

½ cup chicken stock

1   To make the sauce, place the cornflour in a small bowl, then stir in the soy sauce, oyster sauce and stock. Set aside.

2   Heat the oil in a wok or frying pan over a medium heat, add the lamb and stir-fry for 3–4 minutes or until it just changes colour. Remove the lamb from the pan and set aside.

3   Add the onions to the pan and stir-fry for 2–3 minutes. Add the spring onions, garlic and chillies and stir-fry for 2 minutes.

4   Return the lamb to the pan, add the sauce and cook, stirring, for 2–3 minutes or until the mixture thickens slightly. Sprinkle with the coriander and serve immediately.

Serves 4

Note: When handling fresh chillies, don't put your hands near your eyes or let them touch your lips. To avoid discomfort, wear rubber gloves.

Korean Marinated Beef Strips

(see photograph opposite)

500g lean beef fillet, sliced into 5mm thick strips

2 spring onions, chopped, plus extra to garnish

vegetable oil, for brushing

chilli sauce, to serve

MARINADE

2 tablespoons sesame seeds

2 cloves garlic, finely chopped

2½cm piece fresh ginger, finely chopped

2 tablespoons sugar

3 tablespoons light soy sauce

3 tablespoons dark soy sauce

1 tablespoon sesame oil

1 To make the marinade, heat a frying pan, then add the sesame seeds and dry-fry for 5 minutes or until golden, stirring constantly. Grind finely, using a mortar and pestle or a coffee grinder. Add the garlic, ginger, sugar, light and dark soy sauces and sesame oil to the sesame seeds and grind or blend to a paste, using the mortar and pestle or a food processor.

2 Mix together the beef, spring onions and marinade in a non-metallic bowl, turning to coat the beef well. Cover and marinate in the refrigerator for 4 hours.

3 Brush a ridged, cast-iron grill pan or large, heavy-based frying pan with the oil and heat until very hot. Add the beef strips in a single layer (you may have to cook them in batches) and cook for 1–2 minutes, turning once, until browned. Serve with chilli sauce, garnished with spring onions.

Serves 4

Chinese Beef Salad

500g piece fillet steak

2 courgettes

1 red onion

1 red pepper

small salad greens

cress

4 cups cooked rice

pappadums to serve

DRESSING

3 tablespoons black bean sauce

¼ cup peanut oil

1 tablespoon lemon juice

1 Cook steak in one piece in a pan, under the grill or on the barbecue for 20–25 minutes, turning during cooking, or until medium-rare. Leave to cool then cut into 0.5cm slices.

2 Trim ends from courgettes. Using a potato peeler, cut lengthwise strips from courgettes. Peel onion and slice thinly. Cut pepper in half, deseed and cut flesh into thin strips.

3 Toss courgettes, onion, pepper, salad greens and meat together and arrange in four bowls or on plates. Drizzle dressing over salad, garnish with cress and serve with rice and pappadums.

DRESSING

1 Mix black bean sauce, peanut oil and lemon juice together until combined.

Serves 4

Note: For a main dish salad, I usually allow a large handful of small salad greens per person plus a bit more.

Balsamic Pork Stir-Fry

2 teaspoons olive oil

2 cloves garlic, crushed

500g pork fillet, trimmed visible fat, cut into 1cm thick slices

1 red and 1 green pepper, chopped

½ cup orange juice

¼ cup balsamic vinegar

freshly ground black pepper

1 bunch rocket or watercress leaves

1   Heat the oil in a wok over a high heat, add the garlic and stir-fry for 1 minute or until golden.

2   Add the pork and stir-fry for 3 minutes or until brown. Add the peppers, orange juice and vinegar and stir-fry for 3 minutes or until the pork is cooked. Season to taste with pepper.

3   Divide the rocket or watercress among serving plates, and top with the pork mixture. Serve immediately.

Serves 6

Pork and Mango Curry

(see photograph opposite)

1 large onion, chopped

4 cloves garlic, chopped

2 small fresh red chillies, chopped

2 tablespoons curry powder

1 tablespoon sesame oil

1 tablespoon vegetable oil

1 kg pork fillets, cut into 2cm wide strips

2 stalks fresh lemongrass, finely chopped or 1 teaspoon dried lemongrass, soaked in hot water until soft

1 tablespoon Thai fish sauce (nam pla)

2 tablespoons lemon juice

2 mangoes, stoned, peeled and flesh sliced

3 tablespoons mango chutney

1 Place the onion, garlic, chillies and curry powder into a food processor or blender and process to make a smooth paste.

2 Heat the sesame and vegetable oils together in a wok over a medium heat, add the paste and stir-fry for 5 minutes or until all the liquid evaporates.

3 Add the pork and stir-fry for 10 minutes or until the pork is brown. Add the lemongrass, fish sauce and lemon juice and cook over a low heat, stirring frequently, for 15 minutes or until all the liquid is absorbed. Stir in the mangoes and chutney and cook for 2–3 minutes longer or until heated through.

Serves 6

Pork with Pumpkin Stir-Fry

2 tablespoons Thai red curry paste

2 onions, cut into thin wedges, layers separated

2 teaspoons vegetable oil

500g lean pork strips

500g peeled butternut pumpkin, cut into 2cm cubes

4 kaffir lime leaves, shredded

1 tablespoon palm or brown sugar

2 cups coconut milk

1 tablespoon Thai fish sauce (nam pla)

1 Place the curry paste in wok and cook, stirring, over a high heat for 2 minutes or until fragrant. Add the onions and cook for 2 minutes longer or until the onions are soft. Remove from the wok and set aside.

2 Heat the oil in the wok, add the pork and stir-fry for 3 minutes or until brown. Remove the pork from the wok and set aside.

3 Add the pumpkin, lime leaves, sugar, coconut milk and fish sauce to the wok, bring to simmering and simmer for 2 minutes. Stir in the curry paste mixture and simmer for 5 minutes longer. Return the pork to the wok and cook for 2 minutes or until heated through.

Serves 4

Chilli Beef Stir-Fry

2 tablespoon oil

500g lean beef strips

2 teaspoons crushed garlic

1 teaspoon grated ginger

1 tablespoon chilli

2 cups sliced mushrooms

2 tablespoon soy sauce

1 tablespoon cornflour mixed with
  1 tablespoon Chinese wine or
  sweet sherry

4 cups roughly shredded bok choy

1 Heat the oil in a wok over a high heat and stir-fry the beef in batches until golden brown. Remove to a plate.

2 Lower the heat, add the garlic, ginger, chilli and mushrooms and stir-fry for 2–3 minutes.

3 Return the beef to the wok with the soy sauce, cornflour mixture and bok choy and stir well. Cover and cook over a low heat for 3–4 minutes, until cooked. Serve with rice.

Serves 4

Plum and Chilli Beef Stir-Fry

750g lean steak

2 teaspoons olive oil

2 teaspoons freshly crushed garlic

1 onion, cut in wedges, petals separated

1 large courgette, sliced diagonally

1 red pepper, cut into 2½cm cubes

¼ teaspoon ground ginger

1–2 teaspoons hot chilli sauce

½ cup plum sauce

2 teaspoons cornflour

400g can baby corn, drained

370g rice noodles

1   Trim the beef of any excess fat. Slice it into thin strips across the grain. Put a large saucepan of water on to boil for the noodles.

2   Heat the oil in a wok. Stir-fry the garlic and onion for 1 minute. Add the beef in 2 batches and stir-fry for 2–3 minutes. Add the courgette and pepper and stir-fry for 2 minutes.

3   Add the ginger, chilli sauce, plum sauce and cornflour to the beef and vegetables. Add the corn and cook for 2–3 minutes.

4   Meanwhile, cook the noodles in the boiling water for 2–3 minutes.

5   Serve the beef stir-fry with the noodles.

Serves 4–6

Mango and Beef Stir-Fry

340g beef fillet steak, cut into thin strips

2 tablespoon olive oil

3 cloves garlic, crushed

½ teaspoon sambal oelek (chilli paste)

1 tablespoon olive oil, extra

1 red pepper, deseeded and cut into thin strips

8 spring onions, cut diagonally into 3cm lengths

1 tablespoon soy sauce

1 tablespoon sherry

1 teaspoon brown sugar

250g canned mango slices, drained and cut into strips

1 tablespoon chopped fresh coriander

1 Place the beef, oil, garlic and sambal oelek in a bowl, toss well, cover and marinate for 10 minutes.

2 Heat the extra olive oil in a wok over high heat. Add the beef and stir-fry for 3 minutes. Stir in the pepper, spring onions, soy sauce, sherry and sugar and cook for a further 1 minute.

3 Carefully stir through the mango, being careful not to break up the flesh. Add the coriander and serve.

Serves 4

Sliced Steak with Chinese Cabbage

(see photograph opposite)

3 dried Chinese mushrooms

400g lean steak, partially frozen

3 tablespoons peanut oil

2 cloves garlic, chopped

1cm piece of fresh root ginger sliced

1 spring onion, chopped

¼ small Chinese cabbage, sliced

150g baby corn

10–15 water chestnuts, sliced

salt

200ml beef stock

1 tablespoon oyster sauce

1 tablespoon dark soy sauce

2 teaspoons sesame oil

2 teaspoons cornflour

1   Soak the mushrooms in cold water for 30 minutes or until soft. Drain them and remove the stalks before slicing the caps. Cut the steak across the grain into strips 3cm wide.

2   Heat a wok and pour in 2 tablespoons of the oil. Add the garlic, ginger and spring onion. Stir-fry for 30 seconds before adding the steak and mushrooms. Continue to stir-fry until the meat changes colour (3–5 minutes). Remove the steak and mushrooms from the wok.

3   Heat the wok again and add the remaining oil. Stir in the Chinese cabbage, baby corn and water chestnuts. Season the vegetables with salt. Continue to stir-fry for 1 minute before adding the stock. Bring the stock to the boil and cook until the cabbage starts to soften.

4   Return the meat and mushrooms to the wok, add the oyster sauce, soy sauce and sesame oil. Dissolve the cornflour in a little water, and stir it through the meat and vegetables in the wok.

Serves 4–6

Crunchy Veal and Vegetable Stir-Fry

3 tablespoon oil

500g veal escalopes, cut into thin strips

1 tablespoon grated fresh ginger

2 tablespoons chopped spring onions

2 cloves garlic, crushed

¼ teaspoon chilli powder

150g canned baby corn, drained

1 large carrot, cut into very thin strips

60g small cauliflower, cut into small florets

75g peanuts

75g frozen peas, thawed

60g green beans, trimmed

½ cup chicken stock

1 tablespoon soy sauce

2 teaspoon honey

2 teaspoons cornflour, dissolved in 1 tablespoon cold water

1 tablespoon chopped fresh coriander

1 Heat the oil in a wok over a high heat and add the veal, ginger, spring onions, garlic and chilli and stir-fry for 3 minutes. Transfer the veal to a bowl using a slotted spoon.

2 Add the corn, carrot, cauliflower, peanuts, peas and beans to the wok and stir-fry for 2 minutes. Transfer to the bowl with the veal.

3 Reduce the heat, stir in the stock, soy sauce, honey and cornflour mixture and stir until slightly thickened. Return the veal and vegetables to the wok, toss in the coriander and serve.

Serves 4

Veal and Sage Stir-Fry

1 tablespoon olive oil

500g veal escalopes, cut into thin strips

90g chopped prosciutto

½ red pepper, deseeded and cut into thin strips

½ teaspoon cracked black pepper

1 tablespoon fresh sage, chopped

½ teaspoon chilli paste

3 tablespoons white wine

30g spring onions, chopped

1 Heat the oil in a wok over a high heat. Add the veal and fry until golden (about 2 minutes) stirring constantly.

2 Stir in the prosciutto, red pepper, pepper, sage, chilli, wine and spring onions, toss for a further 1 minute and serve immediately.

Serves 4

seafood stir-frys

Prawn, Mange Tout and Mango Stir-Fry

(see photograph on page 68)

1 kg raw peeled medium prawns, defrosted if frozen, rinsed and dried

2 tablespoons vegetable oil

1½ tablespoons finely grated fresh ginger

300g mange tout

bunch of spring onions, sliced

1 large ripe mango, peeled and thinly sliced

2 tablespoons light soy sauce

1 Cut a slit along the back of each prawn with a sharp knife and remove any thin black vein.

2 Heat the oil in a wok, add the ginger and prawns and stir-fry for 2 minutes or until the prawns are just turning pink. Add the mange tout and spring onions and stir-fry for a further minute to soften slightly. Stir in the mango and soy sauce and stir-fry for 1 minute to heat through.

Serves 4

Note: Succulent prawns, crunchy mange tout and juicy mango are flavoured with soy sauce and fresh ginger. Best of all, you can get this dish on the table in 20 minutes. Serve with rice.

Scallops with Courgette in Apple Butter

(see photograph opposite)

2 courgettes, cut into 2½cm thick slices

8 large scallops with their corals

1 tablespoon olive oil

salt and black pepper

⅓ cup apple juice

2 tablespoons butter

fresh flat-leaf parsley, to garnish

1 Turn the courgettes and scallops gently in the oil and season with salt and black pepper.

2 Heat a large heavy-based frying pan until hot, add the courgettes and cook for 2 minutes on 1 side. Turn over the courgettes and add the scallops to the pan. Cook for 1 minute, then turn over the scallops. Cook both the scallops and courgettes for a further minute, until the scallops are golden and the courgettes are browned.

3 Remove the scallops and courgettes from the pan and keep warm. Pour the apple juice into the pan, add the butter and cook until reduced to a syrupy sauce. Spoon the sauce over the scallops and courgettes and garnish with parsley.

Serves 2

Note: Scallops are expensive but delicious, so save this dish for a special treat for two. Make sure you sear them over a high heat; that way they'll be sealed and really tender.

South-East Asian Pan-Fry Prawns

(see photograph opposite)

500g whole raw shell-on prawns,
 defrosted if frozen

3 small red chillies, deseeded and
 chopped

2 cloves garlic, chopped

2½cm piece fresh ginger, chopped

1 shallot, chopped

2 tablespoons peanut oil

1 onion, chopped

2 tomatoes, quartered

1 teaspoon sugar

salt

1 Shell the prawns, leaving the tails attached. Cut a slit along the back of each prawn with a sharp knife and remove the vein. Rinse well, then refrigerate until needed.

2 Blend the chillies, garlic, ginger and shallot to a paste in a food processor or with a mortar and pestle. Heat the oil in a wok or large, heavy-based frying pan over a high heat, then fry the onion for 2 minutes to soften it slightly. Add the paste and stir-fry for 1 minute to release the flavours.

3 Add the prawns and tomatoes, mixing thoroughly, then sprinkle over the sugar and salt to taste. Fry for 3–5 minutes, until the prawns turn pink and are cooked through, stirring often.

Serves 4

Note: It's well worth splashing out on large raw prawns for this spicy dish. But ready-cooked prawns are still tasty and take only a minute to warm through. Serve with rice.

Goan-Style Fish and Coconut Curry

(see photograph opposite)

2 tomatoes

2 cardamom pods, husks discarded and seeds reserved

1 teaspoon each of ground coriander, cumin, cinnamon and hot chilli powder

½ teaspoon ground turmeric

2 tablespoons vegetable oil

1 onion, finely chopped

1 clove garlic, finely chopped

2½cm piece fresh ginger, finely chopped

1⅔ cups can coconut milk

750g skinless white fish fillet, such as haddock or cod, cut into 2½cm chunks

salt

fresh coriander, to garnish

1 Place the tomatoes in a bowl, cover with boiling water and leave to stand for 30 seconds. Peel, then finely dice the flesh.

2 Crush the cardamom seeds using a mortar and pestle. Add the coriander, cumin, cinnamon, chilli powder, turmeric and 2 tablespoons of water and mix to a paste. Set aside.

3 Heat the oil in a large, heavy-based saucepan. Fry the onion, garlic and ginger for 3 minutes or until softened. Add the spice paste, mix well and fry for 1 minute, stirring constantly.

4 Pour in the coconut milk and bring to the boil, stirring. Reduce the heat and simmer for 10 minutes or until the liquid has reduced slightly. Add the fish, tomatoes and salt to taste. Partly cover the pan and simmer, stirring occasionally for a further 10 minutes or until the fish turns opaque and is cooked through, stirring occasionally. Garnish with coriander to serve.

Serves 2

Fragrant Salmon Stir-Fry

250g skinless salmon fillets, cut into strips 2½cm wide and 7½cm long

1½ tablespoon peanut or sunflower oil

1 tablespoon chilled butter, cubed

MARINADE

1 stalk lemongrass, or 1 teaspoon finely grated lemon rind

1 tablespoon soy sauce

½ cup orange juice

1 tablespoon chopped fresh dill

1 tablespoon chopped fresh basil

1 teaspoon grated fresh ginger

1 clove garlic, crushed

salt and black pepper

1 Heat the oil in a large, heavy-based frying pan over a medium to high heat. Transfer the salmon to the pan, reserving the marinade. Cook for 2 minutes, then turn the salmon and cook for a further 1–2 minutes, until cooked through.

2 Arrange the salmon on serving plates. Pour the marinade into the frying pan, bring to the boil, then simmer for 2 minutes. Whisk in the butter and season. Spoon the sauce over the salmon and sprinkle the remaining dill and basil over the top.

MARINADE

1 Peel the outer layer from the lemongrass stalk (if using), then chop the lower white bulbous part, discarding the top. Mix the lemongrass or lemon rind with the soy sauce, orange juice, half the dill, half the basil, the ginger and the garlic, then season. Arrange the salmon strips in a shallow non-metallic dish and pour the marinade over, turning to coat the salmon well. Cover and refrigerate for 2 hours.

Serves 2

Note: A lovely lemon-scented marinade with a hint of ginger caramelises slightly in the pan to make a good thick sauce for fillets of succulent salmon.

Stir-Fry Tamarind Prawns

2 tablespoons tamarind pulp

½ cup water

2 teaspoons vegetable oil

3 stalks fresh lemongrass, chopped, or
2 teaspoons finely grated lemon rind

2 fresh red chillies, chopped

500g medium uncooked prawns,
shelled and deveined, tails intact

2 green (unripe) mangoes, peeled and
thinly sliced

3 tablespoons chopped fresh coriander
leaves

2 tablespoons brown sugar

2 tablespoons lime juice

1 Place the tamarind pulp and water in a bowl and stand for 20 minutes.
Strain, reserve the liquid and set aside. Discard the solids.

2 Heat the oil in a wok or frying pan over a high heat, add the lemongrass or
lemon rind and the chillies and stir-fry for 1 minute. Add the prawns and stir-
fry for 2 minutes or until they change colour.

3 Add the mangoes, coriander, sugar, lime juice and tamarind liquid and stir-fry
for 5 minutes or until the prawns are cooked.

Serves 4

*Note: Tamarind is the large pod of the tamarind or Indian date tree. After
picking, it's deseeded and peeled, then pressed into a dark brown pulp.
It's also available as a concentrate. Tamarind pulp or concentrate can be
purchased from Indian food stores. In oriental cooking it's used as a souring
agent. If unavailable, a mixture of lime or lemon juice and treacle can be
used instead.*

Sautéed Calamari and Vegetables

(see photograph opposite)

2 large calamari tubes

2 teaspoons sesame oil

1 small red pepper, cut into 2cm cubes

2 courgettes, sliced

2 spring onions, chopped

2 teaspoons ground ginger

½ teaspoon minced garlic

3 tablespoons white wine

1 tablespoon lemon juice

2 tablespoons plum sauce

1 teaspoon grated lemon rind

1 teaspoon cornflour blended with
  ½ cup chicken stock

sprigs of Italian parsley

1 Open out the calamari tubes. Score the inside of each tube lightly in a diamond pattern, making cuts 1cm apart. Slice the tube into 3cm squares.

2 Heat the sesame oil in a frying pan and cook the calamari over a moderate heat for 1 minute or until it just starts to curl.

3 Add the pepper, courgettes, spring onions, ginger and garlic and cook for 2 minutes longer. Remove all ingredients from the pan and set aside to keep warm.

4 Pour the wine and lemon juice into the pan and cook for 15 seconds. Add the plum sauce, lemon rind and cornflour mixture and cook, stirring constantly, until the sauce thickens. Return the calamari mixture to the pan and toss to coat.

5 Garnish with a few sprigs of Italian parsley.

Serves 4

Chilli Prawns with Whole Spices

1½ kg green prawns

2 tablespoons oil

1 cinnamon stick

6 cardamom pods

2 whole cloves

½ teaspoon turmeric

2 bay leaves

4 chillies

MARINADE

6 cloves garlic

2 tablespoons chopped ginger

6 chillies

2 tablespoons lemon juice

1 Devein the prawns by cutting the shell along the back and removing the intestine. Wash and dry the prawns.

2 Put the marinade ingredients into a food processor and blend to a sooth paste. Pour the paste over the prawns, cover and marinate for 1–4 hours in the refrigerator.

3 Heat the oil in a wok or frying pan. Add the spices, bay leaves and chillies and cook until the bay leaves change colour. Drain the marinade from the prawns and put it into the wok. Stir-fry until the paste thickens. Add the prawns and stir-fry for 5 minutes or until just cooked.

Serves 6

Stir-Fry Thai Garlic Prawns

2 cloves garlic

2 tablespoons oil

24 raw prawns, tail on, head off

1 tablespoon chopped fresh coriander

THAI DIPPING SAUCE

1 clove garlic

2 sprigs fresh coriander

¼ cup lime juice

½ teaspoon sugar

1 teaspoon Thai green curry paste

½ teaspoon prepared minced chilli

1 Crush, peel and finely chop garlic.

2 Heat oil in a wok. Add garlic and prawns and stir-fry, in batches if necessary, for 1–2 minutes or until just cooked.

3 Serve garnished with coriander and drizzled with or accompanied by individual bowls of Thai Dipping Sauce.

THAI DIPPING SAUCE

1 Crush and peel garlic. Place in a small food processor or blender with coriander, lime juice, sugar, curry paste and minced chilli. Process until garlic and coriander are finely chopped. If you don't have a processor, finely chop garlic and coriander and mix with remaining ingredients until well combined.

Serves 4

Seared Tuna Salad with Crisp Wontons

(see photograph opposite)

DRESSING

½ cup olive oil

¼ cup lime juice

¼ cup orange juice

⅓ cup soy sauce

⅓ cup rice vinegar

1 tablespoon toasted sesame oil

½ bunch fresh chives, minced

1 tablespoon fresh ginger, minced

salt and pepper, to taste

SALAD

1–2 tablespoons peanut oil

1 small red chilli, minced

8 spring onions, finely sliced on the diagonal

100g baby corn

145g mange tout, trimmed

4 tablespoons sesame seeds

4 tablespoons black onion seeds

4 x 145g tuna steaks

salt and pepper, to taste

1 cup vegetable oil for deep-frying

8 wonton wrappers, cut into thin strips

1 To make the dressing, whisk the olive oil, lime juice, orange juice, soy sauce, rice vinegar, sesame oil, chives and ginger in small bowl to blend. Season with salt and pepper.

2 Heat the peanut oil in a wok and add the chilli, spring onions, baby corn and mange tout, tossing over a high heat until the vegetables are crisp tender (about 3 minutes). Transfer the hot vegetables to a bowl and drizzle over a little of the dressing. Set aside.

3 Mix the sesame seeds and black onion seeds on a flat plate and season the tuna with salt and pepper. Press the tuna into the seed mixture, coating both sides evenly. Heat a little more oil in the same wok used for the vegetables. Add the tuna and sear over a high heat until just cooked through. Transfer to a platter and, when cool, use a sharp knife to slice each fillet thinly.

4 Heat some vegetable oil in a wok and, when smoking, add the strips of wonton and cook until golden brown. Remove from the wok and drain on absorbent paper. Add salt to taste.

5 Toss the lettuce leaves with the cooked vegetable mixture and a little more dressing, tossing thoroughly so the leaves are well coated. Add salt and pepper to taste. Divide the lettuce mixture among 4 plates and top with the tuna slices. Arrange a bundle of fried wonton strips on top.

Serves 4–6

Steamed Seafood Mousse

(see photograph opposite)

CURRY PASTE

3 red chillies, chopped

3 cloves garlic, chopped

4 spring onions, chopped

2 tablespoons finely sliced lemongrass

1 tablespoon chopped galangal

1 tablespoon kaffir lime leaves

1 tablespoon chopped coriander

salt and pepper

MOUSSE MIXTURE

125g shelled green prawns, chopped

125g calamari, sliced

1 cup thick coconut milk

2 eggs

125g crabmeat

1 teaspoon thai fish sauce (nam pla)

pinch of sugar

3 cabbage leaves

4 tablespoons basil leaves

2 teaspoons coriander sprigs

kaffir lime leaves, shredded

1 red chilli, sliced

1 Place all the curry paste ingredients in a food processor and add a little water to moisten them. Process until all the ingredients are well blended. Transfer the mixture to a strainer and press out as much moisture as possible (water left in the paste will spit when added to the hot oil).

2 Combine the prawns and calamari in a glass or china bowl and gradually blend in the coconut milk using a large spoon. When half the coconut milk has been added, stir in the curry paste, then blend in the remaining coconut milk. Stir the eggs, crabmeat, fish sauce and sugar into the mousse mixture.

3 Use the cabbage leaves to line a heatproof bowl, then place the basil leaves inside the cabbage leaves. Spoon the mousse mixture into the prepared bowl and cover the mousse with silicone paper or greased greaseproof paper.

4 Pour 5cm of water into the base of a wok and place a wire rack or steamer basket over the water. Bring the water to the boil, then place the mousse in the wok. Cover the wok with a tight-fitting lid and steam the mousse until set (about 20 minutes).

5 To serve, sprinkle the top of the mousse with coriander, lime leaves and sliced chilli. Serve steamed rice separately.

Serves 4–6

Stir-Fry Squid with a Melting Pot of Flavours

250g squid rings

¼ cup cornflour

¼ cup oil

2 cloves garlic

2 shallots

1 teaspoon prepared minced chilli

2 tablespoons brown sugar

2 tablespoons Thai fish sauce (nam pla)

¼ cup vegetarian stir-fry sauce

3 tablespoons lime juice

4 cups cooked rice

1 Toss squid rings in cornflour. Heat oil in a wok or frying pan and stir-fry squid in batches for 1 minute. Remove from wok and set aside.

2 Crush, peel and finely chop garlic. Peel and finely chop shallots. Stir-fry garlic, shallots and chilli for 1 minute in same wok or pan squid was cooked in. Add sugar, fish sauce, stir-fry sauce and lime juice. Bring to the boil.

3 Return squid to wok and heat for 1 minute. Serve immediately on a bed of rice and garnished with fresh basil.

Serves 4

Seafood Risotto with Lime and Chilli

1 stick lemongrass

1 kaffir lime leaf

6 cups chicken stock

1 onion

2 cloves garlic

3 tablespoons oil

1 tablespoon prepared minced chilli

2 cups Japanese rice

3 cups mixed fish, such as prawns,
scallops and cubes of skinned and
boned white-fleshed fish

¼ cup lime juice

1 teaspoon grated lime rind

lime slices to garnish

1 Trim lemongrass and split in half. Crush lime leaf. Place lemongrass and lime leaf in a large saucepan and pour stock over. Bring to the boil and simmer while preparing remaining ingredients. Peel onion and chop finely. Crush, peel and chop garlic.

2 Heat oil in a large saucepan or frying pan. Sauté onion and garlic for 5 minutes or until clear. Add chilli and rice and cook for 5 minutes or until rice is clear. Add 1 cup of chicken stock at a time, discarding lemongrass and lime leaf. Cook, stirring, until stock has been absorbed. Continue until stock is used up and rice is creamy but still slightly firm to the bite.

3 Add fish, lime juice and rind. Fold through rice and cook for 2 minutes or until fish is just cooked. Serve hot, garnished with lime slices.

Serves 6–8

rice and noodles

Noodles with Broccoli and Carrots

(see photograph on page 88)

250g pack stir-fry noodles

3 tablespoons vegetable oil

2½cm piece fresh ginger, finely chopped

2 red chillies, deseeded and finely chopped

4 cloves garlic, finely sliced

2 onions, thinly sliced

2 tablespoons clear honey

1 cup vegetable or chicken stock or white wine

3 tablespoons white wine vinegar

600g broccoli, cut into florets

300g carrots, pared into ribbons with a vegetable peeler

snipped fresh chives, to garnish

1 Prepare the noodles according to the packet instructions, then drain. Heat the oil in a large wok or heavy-based frying pan, then add the ginger and chillies and stir-fry for 1–2 minutes to soften.

2 Add the garlic and onions and fry for 5–6 minutes, until the onions have browned. Stir in the honey and cook for 6–8 minutes, until the honey starts to caramelise.

3 Add the stock or wine and vinegar to the onion mixture. Bring to the boil, then reduce the heat and simmer, uncovered, for 8 minutes or until the liquid has slightly reduced. Stir in the broccoli and carrots, cover, and simmer for 8–10 minutes or until the vegetables are cooked but still crunchy.

4 Stir in the noodles and mix well. Cook, stirring, for 2–3 minutes until the noodles are hot and most of the liquid has evaporated. Sprinkle the chives over the top just before serving.

Makes 6

Chinese Beef and Broccolini Stir-Fry

(see photograph opposite)

400g packet hokkien noodles

⅓ cup blanched almonds

2 tablespoons peanut oil

500g rump steak, thinly sliced

1 onion, sliced

175g sachet Chinese Beef Stir-Fry

2 tablespoons soy sauce

⅓ cup water

1 red pepper, sliced

1 bunch broccolini, cut into pieces

1 punnet baby corn, halved

1 Place the noodles in a bowl of hot water for 1–2 minutes or until the noodles are just tender. Drain and set aside.

2 Dry-fry the almonds in a wok for 1–2 minutes or until golden. Remove and set aside.

3 Heat the oil in the wok. Add the beef and onion and stir-fry for 4–5 minutes.

4 Add the Chinese beef stir-fry, soy sauce, water, red pepper, broccolini and baby corn. Cook for 4–5 minutes or until the vegetables are tender. Add the noodles and almonds and cook until heated through.

Serves 4

Note: Use fresh or dry noodles of your choice. Cook the noodles according to the packet directions or serve with jasmine rice. You can substitute broccolini with baby bok choy or broccoli.

Chilli Mushroom Stir-Fry with Noodles

(see photograph opposite)

15g dried porcini mushrooms

200g fresh Chinese noodles

2 tablespoons sunflower oil

4 cloves garlic, sliced

1 red chilli, deseeded and chopped

2 teaspoons ready-made ginger purée
  or finely grated fresh ginger

500g fresh mushrooms, quartered
  or sliced

4 spring onions, sliced

4 tablespoons rice wine or dry sherry

4 tablespoons dark soy sauce

2 tablespoons lemon juice

1 tablespoon sugar, or to taste

2 tablespoons chopped fresh coriander

1 Cover the dried mushrooms with 75ml of boiling water and soak for
   15 minutes or until softened. Strain and reserve the liquid, then slice the
   mushrooms. Meanwhile, prepare the noodles according to the instructions on
   the packet, until tender but still firm to the the bite, then drain.

2 Heat the oil in a wok or large frying pan until smoking, then add the garlic,
   chilli and ginger and stir-fry for 15 seconds or until they release their flavours.
   Add all the mushrooms and stir-fry for 2 minutes or until softened.

3 Add the spring onions, sake or sherry, soy sauce, lemon juice, sugar,
   coriander, reserved soaking liquid from the mushrooms and the noodles, and
   heat for 1–2 minutes, until warmed through.

Serves 4

Note: The chilli adds extra bite to this oriental mushroom and ginger stir-fry.

Vegetable Stir-Fry with Noodles

(see photograph opposite)

250g pack broad ribbon egg noodles

2 tablespoons sunflower oil

1 garlic clove, sliced

2 carrots, thinly sliced diagonally

150g green beans, halved

150g broccoli florets

1 red pepper, deseeded and cut into matchsticks

4 spring onions, thinly sliced diagonally

chopped fresh coriander, to garnish

lemon wedges, to serve

SAUCE

4 tablespoons smooth peanut butter

1 tablespoon tomato purée

1 tablespoon balsamic vinegar

sea salt and freshly ground black pepper

1 Cook the noodles according to the packet instructions, then drain well.

2 Heat the oil in a wok or large frying pan until very hot. Add the garlic, carrots and green beans and stir-fry for 2 minutes, until lightly coloured. Add the broccoli and stir-fry for 2–3 minutes or until softened. Add the red pepper and spring onions, then cook for a further 1 minute.

3 Add the sauce, 125ml water and the drained noodles. Combine well and stir-fry for 4–5 minutes or until everything is hot. Garnish with the coriander and serve with the lemon wedges to squeeze over.

SAUCE

1 Mix together the peanut butter, tomato purée, balsamic vinegar and seasoning, with about 4 tablespoons of cold water. Set aside.

Serves 4

Note: This stir-fry has a secret ingredient; the peanut butter adds instant sweetness and depth of flavour. You can use whatever vegetables you happen to have in the refrigerator. Like most other nuts, peanuts are high in 'healthy' monounsaturated fats and low in 'unhealthy' saturated fats. They're also an extremely useful source of Vitamin E and zinc.

Lamb Stir-fry with Noodles and Capsicums

225g pack medium egg noodles

2 tablespoons vegetable oil

500g lamb shoulder fillet, sliced into
   1cm pieces

2 carrots, cut into matchsticks

1 red pepper and 1 yellow cpepper,
   deseeded and cut

into matchsticks

200g pak choi, sliced or whole baby
   spinach leaves

200g bean sprouts

4 spring onions, cut into thin strips

4 tablespoons oyster sauce

1 tablespoon dark soy sauce

2 tablespoons clear honey

finely grated zest and juice of ½ lemon

freshly ground black pepper

1 Prepare the noodles according to the packet instructions, then drain well. Meanwhile, heat the oil in a wok or large frying pan until very hot. Add the lamb and stir-fry for 5 minutes, until seared on all sides.

2 Add the carrots and peppers and stir-fry for 4 minutes or until softened. Add the pak choi or spinach, bean sprouts and spring onions, then cook for a further 1 minute.

3 Reduce the heat, then add the drained noodles, oyster sauce, soy sauce, honey, lemon zest and juice and black pepper. Combine well and stir-fry for 2 minutes or until everything is hot and the lamb is cooked through.

Serves 6

Note: It takes a little time to chop everything for a stir-fry, but the cooking time is minimal. This recipe uses the sweet and sour combination of honey and lemon - the result is superb!

Stir-Fried Barbecue Pork with Noodles

340g vermicelli noodles

1 tablespoon sesame oil

250g Chinese barbecued pork, sliced
into thin strips

1 tablespoon grated fresh ginger

10 dried Chinese mushrooms, soaked
in hot water for 20 minutes

1 pepper, deseeded, cut into thin strips

125g mange tout, ends trimmed

45g bamboo shoots, drained and sliced

2 tablespoons honey

¼ cup soy sauce

1 tablespoon red wine vinegar

1 Add the noodles to 4 cups of boiling water and soak until they are al dente.
Drain and keep warm.

2 Heat the oil in a wok over a moderately high heat. Add the pork, ginger and
mushrooms and cook, stirring constantly, for 2 minutes.

3 Add the pepper, mange tout and bamboo shoots and stir-fry for a further
1 minute. Transfer the mixture to a bowl, cover and keep warm.

4 Add the honey, soy sauce and vinegar to the wok and heat until the mixture
boils. Add the noodles to the wok, toss well and serve immediately, topped
with the stir-fried vegetables.

Serves 4

Pad Thai with Pork and Prawns

(see photograph opposite)

250g pack rice noodles

4 tablespoons peanut oil

2 cloves garlic, chopped

1 shallot, chopped

125g pork fillet, cut into 5mm thick
  strips

1 tablespoon Thai fish sauce (nam pla)

1 teaspoon sugar

juice of ½ lime

1 tablespoon light soy sauce

1 tablespoon tomato sauce

200g pack fresh bean sprouts

125g cooked peeled prawns, defrosted
  if frozen

black pepper

60g roasted salted peanuts, chopped

1 tablespoon chopped fresh coriander

1 lime, quartered, to serve

1 Prepare the noodles according to the packet instructions. Drain and rinse
   them. Heat a wok, then add the oil. Stir-fry the garlic, shallot and
   pork for 3 minutes or until the pork turns opaque. Stir in the noodles and
   mix thoroughly.

2 Mix together the fish sauce, sugar, lime juice, soy sauce and tomato sauce,
   then add to the noodle mixture, stirring well. Stir-fry for 5 minutes. Mix in the
   bean sprouts and prawn and stir-fry for a further 5 minutes or until the bean
   sprouts are tender. Season with black pepper.

3 Transfer the mixture to a serving dish. Sprinkle the peanuts and coriander over
   the top and serve with the lime wedges.

Serves 4

*Note: Who can resist this mixture of sizzling pork, lime and seafood? In
Thailand, you can smell the aromas from this dish wafting from the food stalls
that line the streets.*

Nasi Goreng

(see photograph opposite)

250g long-grain rice

1 teaspoon ground turmeric

3 tablespoons vegetable oil

1 bunch of spring onions, thinly sliced

2½cm piece fresh ginger, finely
chopped

1–2 fresh red chillies, deseeded and
thinly sliced

250g pork fillet, trimmed of any excess
fat and thinly sliced

2 cloves garlic, crushed

3 tablespoons soy sauce, or to taste

200g cooked peeled prawns, defrosted
if frozen and thoroughly dried

juice of ½ lemon

fresh coriander, to garnish

1 Cook the rice with the turmeric, according to the instructions on the packet.
Drain, then spread on a large plate. Leave to cool for 1 hour or until
completely cold, fluffing up occasionally with a fork.

2 Heat 2 tablespoons of the oil in a wok or heavy-based frying pan. Add half
the spring onions, the ginger and the chillies and stir-fry over a low heat for
2–3 minutes, until softened. Add the remaining oil, increase the heat to high,
then add the pork and garlic and stir-fry for 3 minutes.

3 Add the rice in 3 batches, stirring after each addition to mix well with the
other ingredients. Add the soy sauce and prawns and stir-fry for 2–3 minutes,
until hot. Transfer to a bowl and mix in the lemon juice. Sprinkle with the
remaining spring onions and garnish with coriander.

Serves 4

*Note: Succulent pork and prawns combine with rice and aromatic spices to
make this simple Indonesian dish. Serve with prawn crackers and plenty of
dark soy sauce.*

Seafood Noodle Stir-Fry

(see photograph opposite)

2 tablespoons sesame oil

1 clove garlic, crushed

2 small red chillies, chopped

1 tablespoon grated fresh ginger

1 kg prepared mixed seafood

½ red pepper, sliced

60g mange tout, cut into 2½cm pieces

250g asparagus spears, cut into
  2½cm pieces

1 tablespoon shredded fresh basil

370g noodles, cooked

1 tablespoon cornflour

¼ cup hoisin sauce

1 cup water

2 tablespoons sesame seeds, toasted

1 Heat the oil in a wok. Add the garlic, chillies and ginger. Stir-fry for 1 minute. Add the seafood, pepper, mange tout, asparagus and basil. Stir-fry until the seafood is just cooked. Add the noodles. Stir-fry for 1–2 minutes.

2 Combine the cornflour, hoisin sauce and water. Stir into the wok. Cook, stirring, until the sauce boils and thickens. Sprinkle with sesame seeds.

Serves 4

Spicy Singapore Noodles

250g rice vermicelli

250g medium prawns

1 tablespoon olive oil

3 cloves garlic, finely chopped

1 tablespoon ginger, minced

3 spring onions, finely chopped

1 tablespoon curry powder

1 onion, thinly sliced

1 carrot, grated

1 red pepper, thinly sliced

125g bean sprouts

125g mange tout, trimmed

SAUCE

½ cup chicken stock

2 tablespoons soy sauce

1 tablespoon sugar

1 tablespoon sesame oil

1 tablespoon rice wine

2 teaspoons cornflour

SAUCE

1 Combine the sauce ingredients and set aside.

NOODLES

1 Soak the vermicelli in hot water for 20 minutes or until softened.

2 Drain and set aside. Peel the shells from the prawns. Starting at the top of the outer curve, cut ¾ of the way through each prawn and open out to butterfly. Discard the vein. In the wok, heat the oil over medium-high heat and cook the garlic, ginger and spring onions, stirring, for 20 seconds or until fragrant.

3 Add the curry powder and cook for 10 seconds. Add the onion, carrot and pepper to the wok and cook, stirring occasionally, for 3–4 minutes or until slightly wilted. Stir in the prawns. Stir the sauce and add to the wok. Bring to the boil. Cook for about 1½ minutes or just until the prawns turn pink. Add the bean sprouts, mange tout and vermicelli; cook, tossing well, for about 2 minutes or until thoroughly heated.

Serves 4

Seafood Noodles with Calamari and Mussels

250g thin egg noodles

½ red and ½ green pepper, deseeded

1 large calamari tube, cleaned

2 teaspoons cornflour

2 tablespoons vegetable oil

salt

black pepper

1 teaspoon crushed garlic

1 teaspoon crushed ginger

1 spring onion, chopped

125g mussels, cooked

8 oysters

1½ tablespoons soy sauce

1½ tablespoons dry sherry

1 In boiling salted water, cook the noodles according to the packet directions until al dente. Rinse in cold water and drain. Cut the peppers into matchstick-thin lengths. Cut the calamari into thin rings. Halve the rings and toss them in the cornflour.

2 Heat the oil in a wok and stir-fry the calamari for 1 minute. Remove, drain on absorbent paper, lightly salt and liberally pepper. Add the garlic, ginger, peppers and spring onion to the wok and stir-fry for 1 minute.

3 Add the seafood, soy sauce, sherry and noodles and stir-fry until heated through. Pile onto a warmed serving dish.

Serves 6

Surprise Rice Parcels

2 cups medium grain rice

2 spring onions

4 shiitake mushrooms

2 double skinless, boneless chicken breasts

¼ cup char siu sauce

4 x 60cm pieces baking paper

4 kaffir lime leaves

1 Cook rice to packet directions.

2 Trim green onions and slice finely. Slice mushrooms. Cut chicken breasts into thin strips. Mix chicken, char siu sauce, spring onions and mushrooms together.

3 Fold each piece of paper in half crosswise. Place a quarter of the rice in the middle of each piece of paper and flatten slightly. Place a quarter of the chicken mixture in the middle of the rice. Place a kaffir lime leaf on top and fold paper to enclose rice.

3 Place in a bamboo steamer and steam for 15 minutes or until chicken is cooked. Serve with a salad of Asian greens.

Serves 4

Note: You can wrap this dish in soaked lotus leaves if wished. They give a delicious flavour to the rice and are available at Asian speciality stores.

Thai Fried Rice

1 cup rice

3 spring onions

12 green beans

1 carrot

2 tablespoons oil

2 teaspoons Thai green curry paste

¼ cup coconut milk

chilli strips

1 Cook rice to packet directions. Drain and spread on an oven tray. Dry in a 150°C oven for 10–15 minutes, turning once.

2 Trim green onions and cut into 2cm pieces on the diagonal. Trim beans and split in half lengthwise. Scrub or peel carrot and cut into very thin lengthwise strips.

3 Heat oil in a wok or large frying pan and stir-fry spring onions, beans and carrot for 2–3 minutes. Remove from wok. Add rice and stir-fry until rice starts to colour slightly. Return vegetables to pan.

4 Mix curry paste and coconut milk together and toss through rice. Serve hot, garnished with chilli strips.

Serves 4

Note: Serve this with grilled or barbecued meats or steamed fish.

Chicken Fried Rice

(see photograph opposite)

4 cups cooked rice

4 rashers bacon

3 spring onions

2 eggs

1 tablespoon sherry

3 tablespoons peanut oil

2 teaspoons grated root ginger

250g chicken tenderloins or stir-fry meat

1 tablespoon soy sauce

1 Spread cooked rice on oven trays and refrigerate, uncovered, overnight. Alternatively, put trays in the sun or in a 180°C oven for 15 minutes to allow rice to dry. Turn rice occasionally.

2 Derind bacon and cut into strips. Trim and finely slice spring onions. Lightly beat eggs and sherry together. Cook bacon in a wok or large frying pan until crisp. Remove from wok and crumble.

3 Heat about one tablespoon of the measured oil in wok and cook half the egg mixture to make a small omelet. Remove from pan and repeat with remaining egg mixture. Cut omelets into thin strips.

4 Heat remaining oil in wok. Sauté ginger and spring onions for 1 minute. Remove from wok and set aside. Add rice and chicken and stir-fry for 5 minutes or until lightly browned. Add bacon, ginger, omelet strips and soy sauce. Heat mixture thoroughly and serve.

Serves 4–6

Note: Any meat can be used instead of chicken for this recipe.

index